Teachers Learning Together

Creating Learning Communities

Adapted from
Coming Together As Readers

Donna Ogle

CORWIN PRESS
A SAGE Publications Company
Thousand Oaks, California

For information:

 Corwin Press
A Sage Publications Company
2455 Teller Road
Thousand Oaks, California 91320
www.corwinpress.com

Sage Publications Ltd.
1 Oliver's Yard
55 City Road
London EC1Y 1SP
United Kingdom

Sage Publications India Pvt. Ltd.
B-42 Panchsheel Enclave
New Delhi 110017 India

ISBN 1-57517-884-2

05 06 07 08 09 10 9 8 7 6 5 4 3 2 1

**CORWIN
PRESS**

The Corwin Press logo—a raven striding across an open book—represents the union of courage and learning. Corwin Press is committed to improving education for all learners by publishing books and other professional development resources for those serving the field of PreK–12 education. By providing practical, hands-on materials, Corwin Press continues to carry out the promise of its motto: **"Helping Educators Do Their Work Better."**

CONTENTS

Teachers Learning Together

Creating Learning Communities

As schools focus on improving student engagement and achievement, bringing together teachers and all others involved in instruction is important. Recent studies of schools that produce student learning well above that expected by their demographics identify teachers who engage together as learners as a key ingredient in their success (CIERA 2001; WestEd 2000; CELA 2000). An analysis of the eight schools that won the Model Professional Development Award from the US Office of Education found that these schools with teachers learning and working together had twice the student achievement gains of comparable schools, despite the level of poverty or transience. The report concluded that "At the heart of each school's success is an exemplary professional development program. . . . Teachers, paraprofessionals, and administrators have coalesced as learning communities and focused their own learning on what will translate into learning for students. Everyone is learning, and everyone benefits" (WestEd 2000, 1).

Creating schools that hum with active learning and are real professional learning communities is challenging. However, there are many resources and professional groups available to support these efforts and increasing numbers of examples of schools that have reaped the rewards of their commitment. All involve some form of collaboration—either within a single school, as part of a larger network of teachers beyond the building level, or as a school-university partnership.

SHARED STAFF STUDY

One of the most natural ways for teachers to come together is to create a learning support team for themselves. A small group learning support team can expand so that shared instructional study becomes a part of the life of the school with staff time devoted to it. Committing to shared staff study is becoming more common. A culture where all teachers are valued and where questions and problems can be openly discussed is by necessity the cornerstone of successful shared learning. Establishing this level of openness and trust may take some time. Different approaches exist to address situations in which such a community has not been established or where it has become dormant.

In resistant settings, it may be easiest for two or three teachers who are interested in continuing their learning to simply make a commitment to one another to establish a regular meeting time together. The teachers select a topic that is of concern to all, and then each can select some articles to read and discuss together. An alternative format is for each teacher to bring in some samples of student work that are of concern and share these with the others in the group on a rotating basis. Getting the ideas and perspectives of other teachers on how to make the instructional activities more effective can be stimulating and, when done sensi-

Getting the Most from Learning Communities

· Use clear, agreed-upon student achievement goals to focus and shape teacher learning.
· Provide an expanded array of professional development opportunities.
· Embed ongoing, informal learning into the school culture.
· Build a highly collaborative school environment where working together to solve problems and to learn from one another become cultural norms.
· Find and use the time to allow teacher learning to happen.
· Keep checking a broad range of student performance data.

(WestEd 2000, 12)

tively, can have lasting effects. With testing being such a dominant part of school life, finding issues and questions to study with a group is not difficult.

Some teachers have consciously taken time to belong to book clubs or literature circles to nurture their own reading and experience the same kinds of shared literacy that is the practice in their classrooms (Daniels 2002). Talking in turn and staying on topic helps teachers understand the reality of literature discussion in their classrooms and helps them identify with students. Talking with students about particular experiences and insights gained in discussing a book with other adults helps make readily apparent one of the joys readers can have throughout life. Even when they are proficient readers, students are often surprised that adults respond differently to texts. Students can get very interested in their teachers' involvement in literacy and ask for stories from subsequent book club discussions.

The popularity of adult book clubs keeps expanding. Daniels reports that in many Chicago schools "we now work to develop simultaneous book clubs of teachers, parents, and kids—sometimes having all these groups read the same book and come together for a festival of sharing" (2002, 6).

Professional Organizations

Association for Supervision and Curriculum Development (ASCD)
    http://www.ascd.org/
International Council on Education for Teaching (ICET)
    http://www.nl.edu/icet
International Dyslexia Association
    http://www.interdys.org
International Reading Association (IRA)
    http://www.reading.org/
Learning Disabilities Association of America (LDA)
    http://www.ldanatl.org/
National Assessment of Educational Progress (NAEP)
    http://nces.ed.gov/nationsreportcard/
National Association for Bilingual Education (NABE)
    http://www.nabe.org/
National Council of Teachers of English (NCTE)
    http://www.ncte.org/
National Education Association (NEA)
    http://www.nea.org/
National Institute of Child Health and Human Development (NICHD)
    http://www.nichd.nih.gov/
National Middle School Association (NMSA)
    http://www.nmsa.org/
North Central Regional Educational Laboratory (NCREL)
    http://www.ncrel.org/
Teachers Applying Whole Language (TAWL)
    http://www.ncte.org/wlu/talk/
Teachers of English to Speakers of Other Languages (TESOL)
    http://www.tesol.org/

INVOLVE A GROUP IN LOCAL AND STATE PROFESSIONAL ORGANIZATIONS

One easy way to help faculty see the value in continued professional development is to involve them in local or state-level professional organizations. For us to grow as professionals, we

Passing On What's Out There

Have a fair of sorts, where publications, conferences, Web sites, and other resources of organizations are reviewed. This coupled with some small incentive (even paying part of the membership or purchasing a school subscription to the association's journals) can bolster the professional identification of the faculty.

should be connected to the larger professional community. A goal of many schools is that every faculty member is a member of at least one professional organization. This insures that there is a continuing inflow of new ideas and perspectives. Being a member of a professional organization is especially important when the faculty finds time to hear reports from those who attend meetings and read the professional journals and share ideas from them.

If your school does not have an active professional identity, begin with some group activities. Make it a social outing to attend a meeting together and then follow up with a discussion of the content of the speaker or workshop. If your faculty has not been involved, this is a good time to encourage them to become members of a professional organization. One of the benefits is that teachers will also receive mail and e-mail communication that will put them in touch with others who are active professionally. It can be a first step in developing awareness of what is available. You could have a fair where publications, conferences, Web sites, and other resources of organizations are reviewed, and then provide incentives for teachers to join.

Use professional organizations' Web sites to find out what is happening, such as what conferences are coming to your area.

Getting Professional Study Groups Started

- Teachers as Reader Groups
- Professional Forums
- Share Instruction with Video Clips

STRUCTURE FOR PROFESSIONAL LEARNING

Professional development needs to be structured to be valuable. Both topics and format need careful planning. There are two basic thrusts for ongoing professional development. The first is to come together around a topic of interest and to meet for a specified period of time. The second is to establish an ongoing conversation among staff based around some framework. Most schools have found that professional discussions need to follow some format for them to be productive. It is too easy for meetings and conversations to lose their focus without a structure.

Several strategies are available to help groups get started.

Teachers as Reader Groups

Many teachers enjoy the opportunity to meet together to discuss books they are reading. A model developed by the Association of American Publishers (Dillingofski 1993) suggests that teachers, principals, librarians, district administrators, and parents meet regularly to read quality children's and adolescent books and an optional professional book. The model they developed suggests that every semester the group of up to ten participants selects at least four quality children's books and one professional book. The group should meet at least six times and have a site coordinator as well as a facilitator to guide the discussion. Books can be selected

Exploring a Topic

One way to structure the exploration of a topic to the best effect is to select one topic and ask teachers to brainstorm their ideas about that topic while a recorder takes notes. Then these ideas can be clustered and topics for the discussion developed around the clusters because they represent what teachers know and are interested in. Questions can be generated from these clusters, too, as the group thinks about their differences and areas of uncertainty.

A second way to foster discussion is to ask two to three of the teachers to prepare ahead of time to talk about the topic for the benefit of the group. After the perspectives of each participant have been presented, the rest of the group can be asked to comment, beginning with "What I liked about these ideas was _____." Follow up with "What I would like to hear more about is _____." With a structure like this for the group to follow, discussion comes more easily and is more focused.

from the IRA Children's Choices or Teachers' Choices or from other annual recommended book lists. Participants in the group make a commitment to read the book prior to the discussion, or if they haven't read the book, then they don't orally participate but just listen during the group meeting.

The discussions flow from reading logs or journals that participants maintain as they respond while reading. These written records of their thoughts provide the basis for the discussions. Participants write their entries about their engagement with the book, commenting on connections they find with the book theme and events, questions that are raised for them by the book, and reflections they make while reading the book. These journal entries provide the starting point for each meeting. After sharing from journals, participants can extend on these ideas orally—and so the discussion evolves.

Professional Forums: Developing a Commitment and Plan

In recent years there have been many hot topics that have served to bring professionals together. Assessments, standards, reduced class size, elimination of reading specialists—the list goes on and on. You can capture these important issues by creating a professional forum for discussion and in-depth exploration of ideas. A way to begin dialogue is to bring teachers and administrators together and discuss ways they want to learn together. Working out some options is useful so there is not a lot of wasted time. Working from a set of ideas allows others to bounce off of them and create something shared, even if the plan that evolves looks nothing like the original proposal. One group of teachers decided to combine reading articles, having some of the teachers share their work, and inviting a speaker from another local district to talk with them.

Share Instruction with Video Clips

If teachers have a level of trust in one another, they can gain a great deal by sharing video clips of their instruction, using them as a point of discussion. Beginning with clips that the teachers are proud of is a way of introducing themselves to one another. Most teachers have no idea how others teach or handle the daily routines of keeping students on track and involving as many as possible in discussions of reading selections. The opportunity to visit other classrooms in this way can be very stimulating. It is hard to find a great classroom snippet, however, so the expectation should not be made too high for what is shared. One of my colleagues and former doctoral students developed a format for sharing based in videos, which works well for teachers (Passman 1999). The structured format makes the teachers comfortable and willing to share.

The results of this kind of focused professional development create an open and rich experience that has expanded to other groups and schools. To learn more, see the Learning Together on Reflective Teacher Practice Groups: Addressing the Human Aspects of Teaching—Building on the Reflective Practice Discussion Group.

Structuring the Sharing of Video Clips

1. At each meeting, one teacher is responsible for bringing a videotape he or she has chosen either to illustrate something that worked well or to illustrate a question or problem.
2. The group views the tape. No one is allowed to comment while the tape is showing.
3. After viewing the tape, each person, except for the teacher on the tape, tells what he or she liked on the tape.
4. Each viewer poses one question about the lesson.
5. The teacher on the tape is then given the floor to comment, both to describe aspects of the lesson and to respond to the questions.

Focus on Student Learning in Discussions

Pat Carini, whose Prospect School was built on a model of teacher descriptive inquiry and shared reflection, has developed guidelines for teachers to engage professionally. Teachers use their own students as the starting point in their reflection of their work as professionals. They focus their teacher lens on the students and write weekly descriptive comments (three to five sentences in length) about each student. Weekly staff development meetings focus around the descriptive review of one student selected by the teacher who was doing the review that week. Teachers share student work, samples, drawings, teacher observations, and weekly comments. For a more complete description of how to learn from student work, consult Himley and Carini's *From Another Angle: Children's Strengths and School Standards.*

Addressing the Human Aspects of Teaching—Building on the Reflective Practice Discussion Group

—Roger Passman

Reflective practice gets much theoretical play in professional development literature, including Berthoff (1987), Cole and Knowles (2000), Grimmett (1988), and Lytle and Cochran-Smith (1992). Yet the sad fact is that little or nothing is done in schools or, for that matter, in colleges of education, to provide either the time or resources for teachers to engage in meaningful reflection. In stark contrast to the norm, I have worked for the past several years with a number of teachers in various school districts, with full administrative support, to build a model for meaningful reflection growing out of the reflective conversation model developed and described by Pat Carini (1986 and 2000). This model focuses teacher discourse on evidence of teaching practice. I call this focused, rule-governed discourse model the Reflective Practice Discussion Group (RPDG) (Passman 1999).

To engage teachers in a reflective discussion about teaching and learning, some RPDG groups use self-created videotapes of participants teaching a lesson as a means for examining pedagogy in action. Other groups choose to focus on student-produced writing to focus their discussion on teaching and learning. The use of a particular teaching exhibit is dependent on the goals of the project. Videotapes are quite useful when the goal of the project is to generally affect teaching styles. When the goal of the project is, however, to have an impact on student performance, then using the student-created products or performances is a good choice. Either approach when matched with the goals and needs of the project can enhance the quality of the discourse.

Reflection Practice Discussion Group (RPDG) Rules

The rules are simple:

- Participants (1) examine the evidence of practice, (2) describe what they observed, and (3) raise questions and speculate about the artifact as the artifact-providing participant listens and takes notes in silence.
- The evidence provider then responds to the prior discussion, answering questions, addressing speculations, and commenting on what he or she found unexpected in the conversation, while the other participants, in turn, listen silently.
- This is followed by a general discussion among all participants centered on what role the evidence plus the discussion plays in teaching and learning.

The RPDG engages teachers in a moderated discussion that, as far as possible, limits the expression of judgment or judgmental comments. Grounded in part on Habermas's (1979) early notions of communicative action and his description of the Ideal Speech Situation (ISS), the RPDG approximates an ISS by creating an environment in which participants engage in mutually beneficial discourse without feeling the need to stake their territorial claims through strategic action. The discussion is moderated. The moderator, generally a respected neutral party not participating in the group discussion, is charged with keeping the discourse on track and reminding participants of the rules. One of the participants supplies the artifacts of practice, either the self-created videotape or samples of his or her students' writing, used to focus the discussion. Each person gets a chance to present an exhibit. This allows each participant to contribute to the process. (See the Reflective Practice Discussion Group Rules sidebar.)

The RPDG is an ongoing process, lasting at least one academic year. A long-term commitment to this process is essential. Conversations at the beginning tend to focus on external problems of teaching, such as blaming the school board, administrators, and the "dreaded" test for the problems associated with teaching. By midyear, participants have begun to internalize their teaching, telling stories about their work. At the end of the school year, participants are engaged in a discourse of progressive change, focusing on their individual ability to support one another while, at the same time, focusing on engaging students. The discourse of blame is all but forgotten. This pattern is similar to that described by Knowles and Cole (1996), in which they identify three patterns of teacher development:

1. *Strategic compliance,* corresponding to early RPDG discourse, is a stage when teachers do no more than comply with demands.

2. *Internalized adjustment,* similar to midstage RPDG conversation, is evidenced by a change in thinking in response to systemic demands, but not necessarily a change in practice.

3. *Strategic redefinition,* paralleling the last phase of RPDG discourse, is evidenced when an individual redefines the dynamics and/or conditions for the context of systemic pressure—a transformation in practice.

Participating teachers value their experiences as members of an RPDG. Florence, a seventh grade social studies teacher, said, "I really didn't want to do it. I was frightened. I didn't want to make the commitment and I didn't want to be on video . . . but I was so glad I did it. It forced me to look at myself on video and I was pleasantly surprised." The idea of the vulnerability incumbent on self-taping her teaching nearly led Florence to not volunteer for the project. Her participation, however, led to an extraordinary change in her performance as a teacher.

Perry, a fifth and sixth grade bilingual teacher, said, "The [RPDG] is probably one of the most single, what can I say, creative experiences that I've had. It's creative because you look at what you're doing and it's examined by your peers . . . and because they're nonjudgmental in their valuation, you really get a good look at what you're doing." Perry found the self- and group examinations to be creatively exciting. His analytic approach forced him to recognize changing practice through others before he saw change in himself.

Focused reflection gives special value and credence to teachers' voices in an authentic and productive way. Both teachers and their students benefit from the encounter.

Teacher Research

Some schools find that teachers prefer to engage in their own classroom research and only come together periodically. The Teachers as Researchers Movement has been popular in some areas, and there is a history and culture of teacher inquiry. If this is not the case in your school, it might be interesting to read the reports of some teacher inquiry projects and see if teachers might like to make a commitment to researching topics of interest. By jointly making a commitment to pursue key topics and questions through teacher research and inquiry, teachers can establish a shared support group to stimulate *and* learn from one another.

Specialists and Teachers Working Together

One important way to increase professional conversations in a school is to rethink the relationship between classroom teachers and specialists. One model that is gaining popularity is to shift reading specialists from a focus only on instruction with special needs readers to having them function as coaches in the classroom, working directly with teachers to provide good instruction. This shift in role takes a great deal of preparation, yet when done carefully, it can be very beneficial to the district.

Because it is clear that working together to improve reading for low-achieving students has positive results, it is worth the time spent in consideration of the emerging shared role of reading specialists.

As a result of a study (Ogle and Fogelberg 2001) of reading specialists who were shifting their roles to work with classroom teachers more directly in classroom settings, nine conditions that support this new working relationship are included in Figure 1. The effectiveness of collaborations between classroom teachers and specialists has led to an increased reliance on such teaming of efforts.

Nine Essential Conditions That Promote Effective Collaborations Between Reading Specialists and Classroom Teachers

1. Administrative Leadership

Principals need to be proactive in helping new partnerships evolve. Assigning students to classes, supporting choice in which teachers work together and how they work together, and providing incentives and resources are just a few of the ways effective administrators facilitate new arrangements.

2. Predictable Schedules and Routines

To make use of additional professionals in classrooms, there must be some regularity to schedules so agreed-upon instructional arrangements can be realized. If special teachers end up sitting in a classroom watching the classroom teacher engage in whole-class instruction, the time is wasted.

3. Flexible Grouping in Classrooms

Added professionals need to be able to work with small groups of students. They can work most effectively in settings where students are comfortable in small flexible groups. When this is the pattern, adults can enter and not disrupt the whole class.

4. New Reading Curriculum, Textbook Adoption, and State Standards

Specialists find they can work easily with teachers as partners, especially when there are new materials and curriculum to be tried. It levels the playing field and creates added reason for all teachers to rethink their instruction and be more open to variations.

Adapted from Donna Ogle and Ellen Fogelberg. Used with permission.

Figure 1

5. Clear Operating Plan

Whenever two or more adults work together, having a clear set of processes and expectations makes life much easier for all involved. Since special teachers cannot be in the classroom all the time, these clear plans permit maximum productivity.

6. Choice in Teaming for Teachers

Because it is challenging for adults to work together, permitting some choice in initial teaming helps ease the changes. It is also true that some teachers never do well in shared settings, and these strong preferences need to be recognized.

7. Variations, Adaptations, and Flexibility

No one form of teaching or teaming works in all situations with all students. With the effort to provide instruction in the regular classroom, there are still times when both students and teachers recognize that taking students into a quieter and less stimulating environment may be most useful. Allowance for variation is crucial for both students and teachers.

8. Adequate Time Frame

Many students, and particularly struggling readers, often need longer blocks of time to engage in their reading activities. So, too, the change process requires time and effort. Therefore, being realistic and providing adequate time frames for both students' and teachers' learning is essential.

9. Open School Culture

For teaming and sharing of instruction to work successfully, teachers need to have an open attitude. School cultures either foster or hinder such sharing. The more the school is characterized as one where teachers learn together, experiment, and share their ideas, the more likely changing and new relationships and responsibilities will be successful.

However, the changes required are significant and all teachers have to expend more effort in learning how to listen and respect one another's priorities and styles of working. Making such new forms of cooperation happen is challenging as well as rewarding.

Professional Literacy Networks

Often reading specialists and teachers at a mature stage in their professional life need to look beyond their own school for a professional development support network where people with similar interests can gather together for learning. One of the first large-scale networks was developed during the early years of Whole Language when teachers who were embracing Whole Language often found themselves as lone voices or at least in a minority in their schools.

The Whole Language Umbrella

Teachers from various other schools who shared their philosophical orientation came together to discuss their instructional concerns, eventually forming Whole Language study groups. The study groups were networked together quite soon into the Whole Language Umbrella, which became a large international network. The study groups served a very valuable function for teachers who wanted to share their ideas and celebrate their successes together. The groups were also a place where teachers kept learning. This network is a great example of what a group of committed teachers can do beyond the regular system.

Suburban Reading Specialists Network

In Illinois, two reading specialists created a Suburban Reading Specialists Network to bring speakers to the Chicago area each year for professional development opportunities. The group meets twice a year for a luncheon and a speech by a prominent reading leader involved in a timely project. With little structure beyond the energy of Lynne Rauscher-Davoust, the luncheons have drawn from two hundred to five hundred people. Members network with other literacy leaders in the northern part of the state. An informal network for nearly twenty years until Rauscher-Davoust took early retirement in 2001, a regional service center of the Illinois State Board of Education and an area reading council have continued the network.

Rutgers Literacy Curriculum network

Dorothy Strickland began a network for curriculum directors and reading specialists years ago as New Jersey State Professor of Reading at Rutgers. In the Rutgers Literacy Curriculum Network, Dorothy listens to the needs of school district leaders, invites speakers to address the members at monthly meetings, and then hosts the meetings and follow-up discussions. Network members have access to a variety of researchers speaking on topics of interest and can keep up-to-date in ways that would be impossible if they worked within their own districts.

Reading Leadership Institute

In the Chicago suburban area, Camille Blachowicz and I created the Reading Leadership Institute (RLI), a spin-off of Dorothy Strickland's idea.

However, because so many speakers come to the Chicago area, the institute's leaders (reading specialists, curriculum specialists, and interested teachers) wanted a format that permitted more discussion among them. Therefore, we have an evolving model that shifts each year. Our first year we surveyed the group to determine the issues they were facing in the schools. We finally focused on reading in grades three to five since most districts felt it was an overlooked part of their literacy and general curriculum. We together developed a survey for the schools, and our members analyzed their own district programs and then shared the results with our group. From there we invited some speakers to talk with us and also began to do some writing about the needs at this level.

Some of the activities of the RLI have included hosting a summer conference that summarizes the theme or topical issue studied that year, bringing in a few key speakers to dialogue with the group, meeting with our Illinois State Board of Education literacy leaders (former Associate Superintendent Eunice Greer and former Special Assistant to the Superintendent Mike Dunn) each fall, and writing a book grounded in the experiences of this group (*Reading Comprehension: Strategies for Independent Learners,* Blachowicz and Ogle 2001).

More forms of professional networks have been evolving, like the Reading Recovery Network and the Early Literacy Network out of Ohio State University. See Learning Together to Support Educational Reform and Change on the Consortium for Educational Change (CEC) as an example of an area network supporting school change.

These networks have developed as a way to bring together teachers and leaders who are engaged in developing a common model of literacy instruction. They hold conferences, have publications, and support the teachers in their networks in significant ways.

If you are not a part of a network and feel the need to reach out beyond your school, look for some group of like-minded and focused professionals and begin your own.

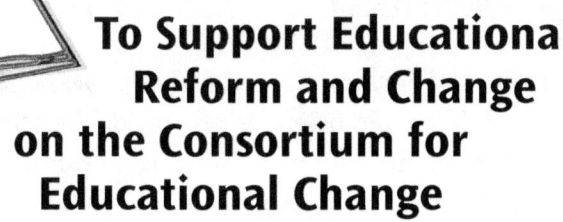

To Support Educational Reform and Change on the Consortium for Educational Change

The Consortium for Educational Change (CEC) is a network of school districts and educational organizations that brings together teachers, administrators, staff, school board members, families, community members, and students. It is an organization that supports educational reform and change through collaboration among these various groups. Membership includes fifty school districts, the Illinois Education Association (IEA), Governor's State University, and National-Louis University (NLU).

CEC grew out of a school council in the Chicago area that, during the 1980s, included a group working on improving labor-management relations. This unique collaboration of members of both labor and management led to discussions about broader educational issues. Participants realized that such an approach could have similarly positive effects on other large-system changes in schools.

CEC provides member districts with a variety of activities to assist in effecting change.

It holds quarterly forums, in panel or presentation format, on current reform topics. CEC sponsors an annual Summer Institute at which representatives from member districts discuss local change efforts and provide planning and sharing opportunities for collaboration. CEC also provides professional development programs for local districts through its Emerging Curriculum. Planners for this curriculum include representatives from the IEA and NLU, a local school board member, and a member-district administrator.

Activities sponsored by CEC are designed so that individuals with different roles in education and different "viewing lenses" can come together to discuss and plan effective change structures in schools. It is hoped that by approaching large-system changes as a team, these groups will have a better chance at long-term success.

SCHOOL-UNIVERSITY PARTNERSHIPS

Many schools find creating and sustaining professional development difficult. It is often helpful to go outside the school and establish a partnership with some other agency or university. These partnerships usually develop when a school or district confronts a particular problem. Many times districts call on professional consultants to work with them on a limited basis. These relationships can develop into long-term partnerships. Productive and highly visible models exist, including those described by Osborne and Schulte (2001), Ogle and Fogelberg (2001), and Ogle and Hunter (2001). The impetus for some recent partnerships has been the need to find ways to include more special education students in the regular classroom. Other partnerships deal with the need to produce higher levels of literacy for all students with an increased focus on assessment and high profile tests.

The Comprehensive Early Literacy Program described in the Learning Together feature evolved from collaboration between reading teachers in Arlington, Virginia, and faculty at the University of Maryland. The project is an example of an extensive collaboration for the improvement of literacy. This project, which lasted five years, began with a broad look at the foundations of literacy and the social contexts in which children become literate.

The Everybody Reads Fluency Project in the Learning Together feature is an example of how such projects develop from real school needs, how resources are found in a university faculty interested in pursuing such problems as developing literacy, and how both groups gain in the endeavor.

Benefiting the Upper Levels

Upper levels, middle and high school, also benefit from professional partnerships with universities. One good example is found in the

Goals 2000 Professional Development Grant to the Chicago Public Schools (CPS). Deans from area universities met with the Division of Staff Development of the CPS at the beginning of this initiative and developed a model that involved each of the universities partnering with five city high schools to improve reading achievement. It focused on cross-curriculum involvement in literacy.

The leadership team in each school, representing the major content areas, met each summer for three years with their university partners to develop their knowledge of the nature of active reading and specific content reading strategies that would help students achieve more in reading. During the school year the team became the leadership group for the school reading committees. The responsibility of the schools was to prioritize reading and have ongoing staff development activities at the school.

One of the strengths of the model was that each of the participating high schools was connected to the university through a doctoral student intern who spent one day a week at the school. It was the intern who helped support the faculty of the high school in initiating changes in the classroom and departmental practices. The intern would often demonstrate teaching or coteaching with the faculty members, attend the reading meetings, and meet with the administration to further their commitment to the project.

The beginning of the project was difficult because there were huge differences in the knowledge and experiences of the teachers and university staff. Most high school teachers assumed that reading was for primary teachers and that reading equaled phonics and decoding. Yet by the second year there was a shared commitment to helping students become strategic readers and learners.

The school that showed the most significant gains (Ogle and Hunter 2001) made reading their top priority for all students and had a strategy of the week that was the responsibility of all faculty to use in their instruction. The principal also used the strategies in his faculty meetings and required that student work be turned in

Learning Together

IN CROSS-INSTITUTIONAL PARTNERSHIPS

The Emergent Reading Strategies Institute's Comprehensive Early Literacy Program

—Janet Steiner O'Malley

John O'Flahavan, a faculty member from the University of Maryland and a researcher with the National Reading Research Center (NRRC), approached the Arlington, Virginia, Public Schools to join with him in an NRRC research project designed to develop a plan for transforming regular classroom instruction for low-achieving students. He was interested in taking some of the findings coming out of the Reading Recovery tutoring model and applying them to classroom instruction to try to accelerate the learning of low-achieving students. We have many schools with high numbers of culturally and linguistically diverse students, so the study had immediate appeal to many in the district, including myself. Because schools and classrooms are busy, complex places, the idea of linking to a university-based teacher-educator project seemed ideal as a way of sorting through the issues that affect kids and teachers. Therefore, I didn't have to think twice about saying "yes" and the same was true for the district. Arlington decided to accept this offer.

Included among the thirty participants were classroom teachers, Reading Recovery teachers, reading specialists, English as a Second Language teachers, district literacy administrators, graduate students, and university professors. Within that group, twenty-one teachers came from four school sites. As we initiated our work together, we reflected on what we thought were the important components of literacy development. We investigated the principles of Reading Recovery (a one-to-one tutorial acceleration program for slow-progress grade one students) and studied the relationship between social contexts for instruction and students' literacy development. We also set four broad goals:

1. Bring together the abilities of local and outside professionals.
2. Develop a framework for a comprehensive literacy program.
3. Evaluate the program.
4. Create a staff development model to suit the needs of teachers in our district.

Throughout the five-year project, the team came together in a variety of ways. Each summer our entire team worked in weeklong sessions to determine future directions and actions and to consolidate learning for the year. These back-to-back, full-day meetings accelerated what the team was able to accomplish. During the school year, the members also held monthly total team meetings. These meetings usually ran for two to three hours either after school or during school, with release time provided by the district. The monthly meetings helped sustain the focus on the theme: change.

The school-based teams met as often as each chose, to support one another and to promote change within their respective buildings. In these meetings, we made a strong effort to get past the talk and into action. The teams problem solved, peer coached, modeled, brainstormed, and conducted workshops. The university-based researchers, who were former teachers for the most part, collaborated with us on new ideas and actions. The university researchers videotaped events, took field notes, and shared information with the participants between the monthly meetings.

District literacy administrators supported the work. They kept current with participants' change by attending team meetings. Through their efforts, the project received funding for summer sessions, increased release time during school, and additional student reading material in classrooms. Also, they supported a staff development model that evolved out of the project by providing funding for planning and instruction, textbooks, and recertification points for participants.

The team started our inquiry by looking closely at the principles of Reading Recovery to see how they might inform our regular classroom instruction. We talked a lot about the social nature of learning, videotaped instruction, analyzed our interactions, and learned to think differently along the way. The dynamic nature of inquiry proved fascinating. Once John tossed the first question into the water, its effect rippled on and on. One question generated many other questions, answers, and understandings. Those involved came to value what seemed like reaching a dead end because unexpected learning always came from having to change direction and action. Meaning developed from the feeling of chaos stimulated by John's strategy of always questioning the participants' assumptions and practices.

We also evolved innovative group contexts for students to socially construct their strategy use. This was an essential starting place without which analysis of individual practice and the understanding of how theory and practice relate could not have been realized. In time the team identified components of a supportive literacy environment, documented students' ongoing development, and analyzed the use of reading strategies by specific students. Then the team balanced the literacy environment by adding more components and evolved the Framework for a Comprehensive Early Literacy Program.

The components of the framework include:
- continuous assessment of individual progress
- reading to, with, and by children
- writing to, with, and by children
- talking to, with, and by children
- activity centers for developing collaboration, independence, and autonomy
- embedded word studies
- home-school interfaces
- safety net interventions for students who fail to achieve on the school's schedule
- coordinated program and staff development structures

Each of the nine components features literacy in differing yet complementary ways.

A group of us Reading Recovery teachers developed and disseminated an emergent literacy framework to other teachers in the district. Among the outcomes of this effort was a movement throughout Arlington toward strategy-based instruction, word studies embedded in the language of the classroom, and instructional decision making that is grounded in developmental theory. To help deepen this understanding across the district, the team created a staff development course. The ongoing model, the Emergent Reading Strategies Institute (ERSI), offers ten three-hour class sessions through which participants earn recertification credit upon completing course requirements. Admission to the institute is so popular that two simultaneous institutes were created to absorb the long waiting list. The course continues to evolve as more is learned both locally and from the larger professional community. In addition, ESL and upper-level and special education teachers have also asked to be included, which has helped shape the course. Some principals have also taken the course, and as they hire new teachers from within the district, they prefer those teachers who have been part of the ERSI course.

Everyone involved in the project gained a broader and deeper understanding of early literacy development. The Framework for a Comprehensive Early Literacy Program has been shared with other districts. By the end of our project, the participants understood that their design was relevant to upper-grade students as well.

The cross-institutional partnership allowed professionals to come together to bring about sustained and ongoing reflection and change in our instructional program. The university partners brought great perspective, which was invaluable to the success of the project.

Everybody Reads Fluency Project—A Teacher Research Group Success Story

The Everybody Reads Fluency Project grew from one school district's interest in readers at the low-middle achievement level—students who knew how to read but struggled with rate and accuracy. Faculty at National-Louis University (NLU) were interested in putting into practice in classrooms clinical findings about fluency instruction. The project was a collaboration between Evanston-Skokie School District 65 in Evanston, Illinois, and NLU to develop a group of teachers and community volunteers to improve reading instruction and reading achievement in the elementary schools.

Reading fluency is the ability to read at a good rate, with good accuracy, intonation, and phrasing. Research has shown that fluency is an accurate measure of overall reading performance and fluency practice in itself is effective in helping struggling readers improve their reading skills. In the first year, one teacher leader from each of thirteen schools and several NLU facilitators met monthly. They studied the research on fluency and developed instructional methods for building students' reading fluency. They learned a quick assessment method for creating a "fluency snapshot" of the class. Using this information, teachers planned and implemented reading activities involving both large and small group instruction.

That summer, a steering group of teachers made a handbook of ways for teachers to put a fluency spin on their language arts instruction.

The second year the project included an additional teacher from each school, a volunteer coordinator, and fifty plus community volunteer tutors. While teachers met monthly with facilitators to share activities, results, and ideas, volunteers were trained in repeated reading, a strategy to improve fluency. Volunteers were placed in teachers' classrooms, where they worked with four identified students twice a week. As students saw their reading rate and accuracy improve during each tutoring session, their motivation for reading increased dramatically. Pre- and post-assessments showed significant gains in students' fluency over the year.

After two years, teacher leaders and NLU faculty created handbooks and videotapes for ongoing staff development. (See the Illinois State Board of Education Web site at http://www.illinois-reads.com/.) Staff development and volunteer training continues, led by teacher leaders, the district literacy director, and a volunteer coordinator. More than seventy additional teachers and community volunteers have joined the project to learn strategies for improving students' reading skills through fluency practice.

with faculty lesson plans. Furthermore, the principal arranged for temporary assigned teachers and those needing help to attend Saturday staff development classes in reading offered at the school.

In each of the schools, there were common elements that led to their successes:

- Each school developed a shared commitment to content reading and made it a priority for all departments.
- Each school supported the development of new strategies on the part of the faculty.
- Each school created an infrastructure that could sustain their efforts.

In two of the schools, the university interns continued to work as part of the school teams: one was hired as the reading specialist and another has continued as a consultant and now works for the central high school division. This partnership proved advantageous for the public schools and the university faculty and students in a variety of ways. It provided a context for the university faculty member to partner with administrators and teachers and test out ideas (Ogle 2000) and provided a field site for doctoral students to also gain skills and conduct doctoral research (Boran 2000). The schools gained by having an ongoing relationship with reading professionals willing to listen and partner in dealing with real problems.

JUST SAY "YES"

Being aware of our own continuing participation in adult shared reading activities and groups, and sharing that with our students, helps keep fresh the ongoing roles reading can play in all our lives. Most adults read on the job regularly (Smith 2000) for learning, for keeping up with our colleagues' activities, and for reinforcement. Helping students know about the benefits of being good readers is one of our responsibilities. We can do this in a variety of ways, only a few of which have been suggested here.

The enthusiasm engendered through cooperative relationships is aptly communicated by Janet Steiner O'Malley, whose district took part in the university-district partnership that developed the Comprehensive Early Literacy Program:

> If the opportunity comes your way, just say yes. Each of us has nagging questions about the decisions we must make in our classrooms; but we cannot easily get to the answers. Life there is fast paced and we have our minds on half a dozen things at the same time, and we're on our own. There seems to be a ceiling effect to how much we can learn if we keep to ourselves. That's why, at school when we need help, we go to a colleague who will lend us a perspective or an expertise that adds to our understanding; we need each other to learn and accomplish things. It's essential to be able to come together with others who share the same interest in the same questions with efforts structured for sustained learning to occur.

BIBLIOGRAPHY

Blachowicz, C., and D. Ogle. 2001. *Reading comprehension: Strategies for independent learners.* New York: Guilford Press.

Berthoff, A. E. 1987. The teacher as researcher. In *Reclaiming the classroom: Teacher research as an agency for change,* (pp. 28–38), edited by D. Goswani and P. R. Stillman. Portsmouth, NH: Boynton/Cook.

Boran, K. 1999. Rising from the ashes: A dramaturgical analysis of teacher change in a Chicago public high school after probation. Doctoral dissertation. National-Lewis University.

Calkins, L. 2001. *The art of teaching reading.* New York: Longman.

Carini, P. 1986. Prospect's documentary process. Bennington, VT: The Prospect School Center.

———. 2000. Prospect's descriptive process. In *From another angle: Children's strengths and school standards/The Prospect center's descriptive review of the child,* (p. 8–22), edited by Himley and P. F. Carini. New York: Teachers College Press.

Carson, B. S. and C. Murphey. 1996. *Gifted hands.* Grand Rapids, MI: Zondervan Publishing.

Collins, D. 1997. *Achieving your vision of professional development: How to assess your needs and get what you want.* Greensboro, NC: Serve.

Cooke, G. J. 2002. *Keys to success for urban school principals.* Arlington Heights, IL: SkyLight Professional Development.

Cullinan, B. E. 2000. *Let's read about: Finding books they'll love to read,* (2nd ed.). New York: Scholastic.

Cunningham, A. E., and K. E. Stanovich. 1998. What reading does for the mind. *American Educator,* (Spring-Summer), 8–17.

Cunningham, P., D. Hall, and M. Defee. 1998. Nonability-grouped, multilevel instruction: Eight years later. *Reading Teacher,* 51(8): May, 652-64.

Daniels, H. 2002. Literature circles: Voice and choice in book clubs and reading groups. Portland, ME: Stenhouse.

Darling-Hammond, L. 1996. Teaching and America's future: Report of the Natinal Commission and America's Future. New York: National Commission on Teaching & America's Future.

Edwards, P. and J. Danridge. 2001. Developing collaboration with diverse parents. In *Collaboration for diverse learners: Viewpoints and practices,* (pp. 251–274), edited by V. Risko and K Bromley. Newark, DE: International Reading Association.

Habermas, J. 1979. *Communication and the evolution of society.* (T. McCarty, Trans.). Boston: Beacon Press.

Himley, M., and P. F. Carini, eds. 2000. *From another angle: Children's strengths and school standards.* New York: Teachers College Press.

International Reading Association. 2000. *Making a difference means making it different.* IRA pamphlet. Washington, DC: International Reading Association.

Kennedy, T., and G. Canney. 2001. Collaboration across language, age, and geographic borders. In *Collaboration for diverse learners: Viewpoints and Practices,* (pp. 310–329), edited by V. Risko and K. Bromley. Newark, DE: International Reading Association.

Kessler, R. 2000. *The soul of education: Helping students find connection, compassion, and character at school.* Arlington, VA: Association for Supervision and Curriculum Development.

Klooster, D., J. Steele, and P. Bloem. 2001. *Ideas without boundaries: International educational reform through reading and writing for critical thinking.* Newark, DE: International Reading Association.

Mulhall, C. 1997. Finding time for faculties to study together. *Journal of Staff Development,* 18(3): 29–32.

Noddings, N. 1992. The challenge to care in schools: An alternative approach to education. In *Advances in Contemporary Educational Thought,* Volume 8. New York: Teachers College Press.

Ogle, D. 2000. Make it visual. In *Creativity and Innovation in content reading and learning,* (pp. 103–114), edited by McLaughlin, M., and M. E. Vogt. Norwood, MA: Christopher Gordon.

Ogle, D., and K. Hunter. 2001. Developing leadership in literacy. In *School leadership in times of urban reform,* (pp. 179–194), edited by M. Bizar and R. Barr. Mahwah, NJ: Lawrence Erlbaum Associates.

Organization for Economic Development. 2001. The Report of the PISA Study. Washington, DC: Organization for Economic Co-Operation and Development.

Osborne, S. S., and A. C. Schulte, 2001. A school-university project on collaboration and consultation. In *Collaboration for diverse learners: Viewpoints and practices,* (pp. 330–347), edited by V. Risko and K. Bromley. Newark, DE: International Reading Association.

Passman, R. 1999. Discussion focusing on a developing student-centered practice with four middle-level school teachers. Unpublished Doctoral Dissertation. National-Lewis University.

Perez, B. 2001. Communicating and collaborating with linguistically diverse communities. In *Collaboration for diverse learners: Viewpoints and practices,* (pp. 231-250), edited by V. Risko and K. Bromley. Newark, DE: International Reading Association.

Raphael, T., and S. I. McMahon. 1994. Book club: An alternative framework for reading instruction. *The Reading Teacher,* 48: 102–116.

Rasinski, T. V., et al. 2000. *Teaching comprehension and exploring multiple literacies: Strategies from the reading teacher.* Newark, DE: International Reading Association.

Risko, V., and K. Bromley. (Eds.). 2001. *Collaboration for diverse learners: Viewpoints and practices.* Newark, DE: International Reading Assocaition.

Rodriguez-Brown, F. 2001. Home-school connections in a community where English is the second language: Project FLAME. In *Collaboration for diverse learners. Viewpoints and practices,* (pp. 273–288), edited by V. Risko and K. Bromley. Newark: DE: International Reading Association.

Schoenbach, R., C. Greenleaf, C. Cziko, and L. Hurwitz. 1999. *Reading for understanding: A guide to improving reading in middle and high-school classrooms.* San Francisco: Jossy-Bass Publishers in partnership with WestEd.

Stigler, J. and J. Hiebert. 1999. *The teaching gap: Best ideas from the world's teachers for improving education in the classroom.* New York: The Free Press.

Strickland, D. 1993. Networking for change: The Rutgers Literacy Curriculum Network. *Primary Voices K–6,* 1(2): 1–6.

Trealease, J. 2001. *The read-aloud handbook,* (5th ed.). New York: Penguin.

WestEd. 2000. *Teachers who learn, kids who achieve: A look at school with model professional development.* San Francisco, CA: WestEd.

NOTES

NOTES

NOTES

NOTES

In compliance with GPSR, should you have any concerns about the safety of this
product, please advise: International Associates Auditing & Certification
Limited The Black Church, St Mary's Place, Dublin 7, D07 P4AX Ireland
EUAR@ie.ia-net.com

www.ingramcontent.com/pod-product-compliance
Lightning Source LLC
Jackson TN
JSHW080038010226
97517JS00015B/164